great songs... for weddings

edited by **milton okun**

ISBN-13: 978-1-57560-956-0
ISBN-10: 1-57560-956-8

Visit our website at www.cherrylane.com

INTRODUCTION

Of all the institutions affected by the social and emotional changes of the last few decades, none has remained intact as much as the traditional wedding. From the food and the venue to the color of the napkins and the size of the guest list, men and women alike are still consumed by this looming event throughout the entire engagement period. But with a lifetime of memories at stake, few elements of the wedding are more significant than the nature and the presentation of the music.

Today's wedding is often a virtual mixed CD. While an adept and sympathetic deejay or specialized dance band is usually hired to handle the task of keeping the guests suitably entertained during the pre- and post-ceremony hours, several key songs are still within the sole province of the family. The bride's dance with her father is always an emotional highlight. Traditionally, this has been a song selected by Dad as he sends his daughter off into a new phase of her life. Whether the song is meant to celebrate the ending of an era or to reflect on the passage of time or the emotional changing of the guard, it is a deeply personal choice. In this context, romantic ballads like Joe Cocker's "You Are So Beautiful" and the Commodores' "Three Times a Lady" can bring the assemblage to tears. Recently, however, daughters have been taking the opportunity to use songs like "The Wind Beneath My Wings" to make a statement of thanks to the proud papa, for bringing her to this moment, literally and figuratively.

The groom's dance with his mother is generally not quite so sentimental, although there is certainly room for important feelings to be shared. It might be the perfect time for a touch of the philosophical, like John Denver's eloquent "Perhaps Love" or Jimmy Durante's timeless "Make Someone Happy." If something a bit more festive is desired, Elton John's "Can You Feel the Love Tonight" conveys an inclusive and universal message. The Bill Withers duet with Grover Washington Jr., "Just the Two of Us"—which Will Smith updated when he sang it to his son—can work equally well with mother and son.

By far the most profound and personal moment in the wedding celebration is the bride and the groom's first dance as husband and wife, which, by focusing everyone's undivided attention on the happy couple, is certain to be the musical highlight of the entire event. Whether the wedding itself will be held in the home of the parents or on a scenic mountaintop in Maui, this first dance is what all the guests will remember for years to come—and why a book like this is not only entertaining, but essential.

From the winsome innocence of "We've Only Just Begun" and "This I Promise You" to the more mature proclamations of "One in a Million You," "The Glory of Love," "Don't Know Much," and "Tonight I Celebrate My Love," the songs collected in these pages represent the best popular wedding songs of several generations. These are songs that have stood the test of time, and more importantly, the test of repeated weddings. Even so, there is remarkable diversity here, ranging from show tunes like "A New Life" (Jekyll & Hyde) and "It's Your Wedding Day" (The Wedding Singer) to arena ballads like Journey's "Open Arms" and Foreigner's "Waiting for a Girl Like You." Also included are Oscar-winning movie titles, classic standards, chart-topping pop tunes, reflective singer/songwriter odes, country songs, grown-up rhythm and blues, and the all-time wedding classic "May You Always." There is more than enough to reflect a cross-section of attitude, style, and taste as vast as music itself.

For sophisticated types planning a conservative wedding, there are chestnuts like Nat King Cole's poignant "Unforgettable" and Frank Sinatra's "The Way You Look Tonight." The great emotional powerhouse "At Last," by Etta James, is sure to provoke a tear. Rod Stewart has recently joined the ranks of wedding balladeers, putting a contemporary stamp on "Have I Told You Lately."

For a majestic approach, filled with pomp and circumstance, could there be anything finer than "When I Fall in Love" as done by Celine Dion and Clive Griffin or "I Finally Found Someone" by Barbra Streisand and Bryan Adams? For a simpler affair in the backyard, with a much more relaxed pace, a country tune could be the perfect answer. Some of the best modern country songs are included here. In choosing Lonestar's lovely "Amazed," Anne Murray's "Could I Have This Dance," John Michael Montgomery's heartfelt "I Swear," or Eddie Rabbitt's simmering duet with Crystal Gayle "You and I," you can be sure the genuine sweetness of the emotions will shine through. Then again, "Can't Help Falling in Love," by the immortal Elvis Presley, who has recently made a comeback on the pop charts, could accomplish the rare feat of uniting several generations around a single song.

Decisions like this are what shape a great and memorable wedding and reception. Coming together over the music for this sacred gathering can provide an opportunity for intimacy and sharing between the future bride and groom—as well as between the families—unequalled by any of the other more mundane details. What better way to peer into another's soul than through music?

But the joy of this book is not only to be found prior to the wedding ceremony. With the words and the music to all these great love songs together in one place, an added pleasure of having a volume like this around the house is that it enables a couple to memorize, play, and sing wonderful love songs like "Endless Love" or "(I've Had) The Time of My Life" to each other for many years to come.

—Bruce Pollock

Bruce Pollock is the author of *When the Music Mattered: Rock in the 1960s* and *The Rock Song Index: The 7500 Most Important Songs of the Rock and Roll Era, 1944-2000.*

CONTENTS

Against All Odds (Take A Look At Me Now)

Words and Music by Phil Collins

Recorded a half step lower.

on - ly one who real - ly knew me ___ at all. ___

How can you just walk a - way from me, when all I can do is watch you leave? ___ 'Cause we've
wish I could just make you turn a - round, turn a - round and see me cry. ___ There's so

shared the laugh - ter and ___ the pain, ___ and e - ven shared ___ the tears. ___ You're the
much I need ___ to say ___ to you, ___ so man - y rea - sons why. ___ You're the

well, there's just an emp-ty space, _____ and you com-ing back _____
'cause there's just an emp-ty space. _____ But to wait _____

_____ to me _____ is a - gainst _____ the odds, _____ and that's what _____ I've got _____ to face. _____
_____ for you _____ is all _____ I can do, _____ and that's what _____

I _____ I've got _____ to face. _____ Take a good look at me now, _____

'cause I'll still be stand-ing here, and you com-ing back to me is a-gainst all odds, it's the chance I've got-ta take.

Take a look at me now.

8

All My Life

Words and Music by Karla Bonoff

I nev-er thought_ that I could feel _ a love so ten-der; I nev-er thought_ I could let those feel-ings show. _____ But now my heart is on _ my sleeve, and this love will nev-er leave. I _ know,_ I know.

D.S. and fade

11

All My Life

Words by Joel Hailey
Music by Joel Hailey and Rory Bennett

Original key: D♭ major. This edition has been transposed down one half-step to be more playable.

I will nev-er find an-oth-er lov-er sweet-er than

you, sweet-er than you. ___ And I will nev-er find an-oth-er

lov - er more pre - cious than you, _____ more pre - cious than you. _____ Girl, you are

close to me, you're like my moth - er, close to me, you're like my fath - er, close to me, you're like my sis - ter,

close to me, you're like my broth - er. You are the on - ly one. _____ You're my ev -

- 'ry - thing and for you _____ this song _____ I sing. _____ all my life _____
And

feel the same ___ way too. _____ Yes, I

pray that ___ you do love ___ me too. _____ I said you're

all _____ that I'm think - ing of. _____

Da, da, da, da, da. Da, da, da, da, da. Da, da, da, da, da. Da, da,

da, da, da. Said I prom-ise to nev-er fall in love ___ with a strang-er.

You're all I'm think-ing of. I praise the Lord a-bove for send-ing me your love.

I cher-ish ev-'ry hug. I real-ly love you.

D.S. al Coda

For

CODA

do love ___ me. You're all _____ that _____ I ev -

When you smile life is glow. You picked me up when I was down. And I

hope that ___ you feel the same ___ way too. ___

___ Yes, I pray that ___ you do love ___ me

too. ___ In all my life ___

I prayed for some-one ___ like you and I thank God ___ that ___ I, that I fin-al-ly found ___ you. ___ For all my life ___

Repeat and Fade

I prayed for some-one ___ like you. Yes, I

Optional Ending

you.

20

Amazed

Words and Music by Chris Lindsey,
Marv Green and Aimee Mayo

Moderately slow Country Ballad

With pedal

The Ev-'ry time our eyes meet, this feel-in' in-side me
The smell _ of _ your skin, the taste _ of your kiss,

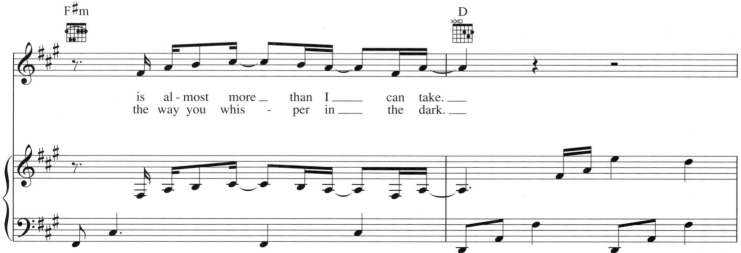

is al-most more _ than I _ can take. _
the way you whis - per in _ the dark. _

*Recorded a half step lower.

ba-by, I'm a-mazed by you.

ba-by, I'm a-mazed by you.

Ev-'ry lit-tle thing that you do. _

I'm so in love _ with you. _ It just keeps get-tin' bet - ter. _

I wan-na spend the rest of my life _____ with you by my side _____ for-ev-er and _ ev - er. Ev-'ry lit-tle thing that you do, _ oh, _____ ev-'ry lit - tle thing that you _ do, _____ ba-by, I'm a-mazed _ by _ you.

Freely

Tempo I

Always And Forever

Words and Music by Rod Temperton

Lyrics:
Al-ways and for-ev-er, _____ each mo-ment with
There'll al-ways be sun-shine _____ when I look at

you
you.
is just like a dream to _____ me _____
It's some-thing I can't ex-plain, _____

27

own spe - cial way, melt all my heart a -

way ____ with a smile. ____ Take time to

tell me ____ you ____ real - ly care ____ and

we'll share ____ to - mor - row ____ to - geth - er. ____

Annie's Song

Words and Music by John Denver

At Last

Lyric by Mack Gordon
Music by Harry Warren

Oh, _____ yeah, ___ yeah. ___ At ___ last,

the skies _ a - bove _ are blue. ___ My _ heart _ was wrapped up

in clo - ver the night I _____ looked at you.

I found a dream that I could speak to, _____ a dream that

35

and here __ we are _____ in heav - en,

for __ you are mine _____ at __ last.

Beautiful In My Eyes

Words and Music by Joshua Kadison

Can You Feel The Love Tonight

Music by Elton John
Lyrics by Tim Rice

wide - eyed ___ wan - der - er   that we   got this far. ___

And can   you feel ___ the love ___

___   to - night, _____   how it's laid ___ to rest? ___

___   It's e - nough _____ to make

from the Paramount Picture BLUE HAWAII

Can't Help Falling In Love

Words and Music by George David Weiss,
Hugo Peretti and Luigi Creatore

Slowly, steadily

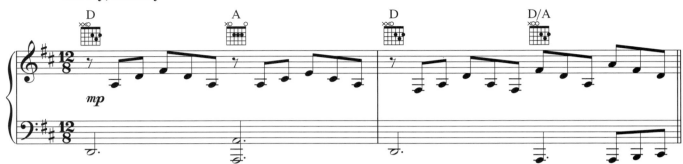

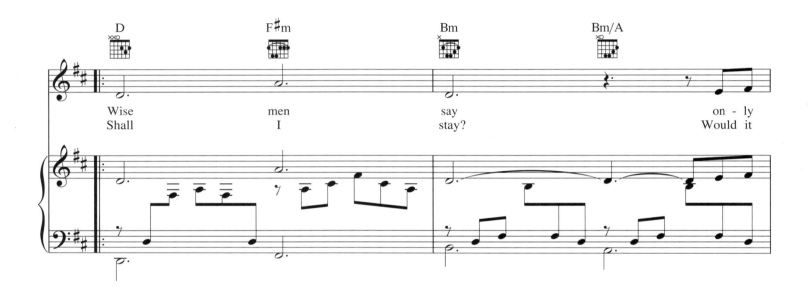

Wise   men   say   on - ly
Shall   I   stay?   Would it

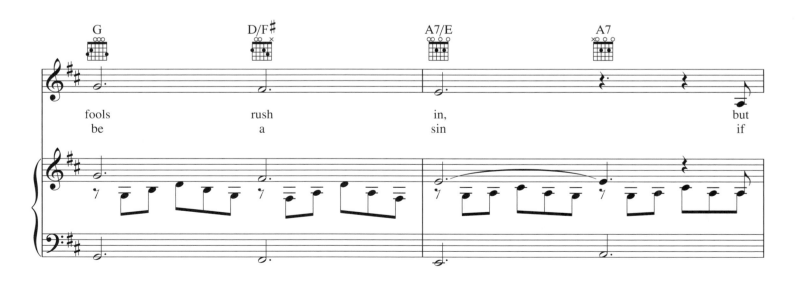

fools   rush   in,   but
be   a   sin   if

some things ___ are ___ meant to be.

Take my hand, take my

whole life too, for

I can't help fall - ing ___ in

48

from URBAN COWBOY

Could I Have This Dance

Words and Music by Wayland Holyfield and Bob House

52

from the Motion Picture ROBIN HOOD: PRINCE OF THIEVES

(Everything I Do)
I Do It For You

Words and Music by Bryan Adams,
Robert John Lange and Michael Kamen

Don't Know Much

Words and Music by Barry Mann,
Cynthia Weil and Tom Snow

that may be _____ all I need ___ to know.

So man - y ques - tions still left un - an - swered.

So much I've nev - er bro - ken through. _____

But when I feel you near me some - times I see so clear - ly.

and that may be _____ all I need ___ to

know.

I don't know ___ much,

but I know I love you, _____ and

from ENDLESS LOVE

Endless Love

Words and Music by
Lionel Richie

Moderately slow

My love, ___ there's on - ly you in my life, ___
Two hearts, ___ two hearts that beat as ___ one; ___

the on - ly thing that's right. ___
our lives have just be - gun. ___

My
For-

first ___ love, ___ you're ev - 'ry breath that I take, ___
ev - er, ___ I'll hold you close in my arms, ___

they tell me how much   you   care.
you mean the   world   to   me.
Oh,
Oh,

yes,   you will   al -   ways   be
I know   I've found   in   you

my   end - less   love.
my   end - less

love.

Oh, _____ and _ love, _____

cresc.

mf

I'll be that fool for _____ you, _____ I'm _____ sure; _____ you _____ know I don't mind. _____ And yes, _____ you'll be the on - ly ___ one. _____ No one can de - ny _

this love _____ I have in-side. I'll

give _____ it all to you, my love, _ my love, _

_____ my end-less love.

from the Spelling Television Series BEAUTY AND THE BEAST

First Time I Loved Forever

Words and Music by Lee Holdridge and Melanie Safka

first time I loved for - ev - er _____ was when you whis - pered my name. And I

knew at once you loved me _____ for the me of who I am.

The first time I loved for - ev - er ___ I
cast all else a - side. And I bid my heart to fol - low, ___ be there
no more need to hide.

cresc. e accel.

Slightly faster

And if wish - es and dreams are mere - ly for chil - dren, and if love's a tale for
fools, ___ I'll live the dream with you. ___

For all my life and for-ev-er,_____ there's a truth I will al-ways know. When my world di-vides and shat-ters,_____ your_ love is where I'll go.

Follow Me

Words and Music by John Denver

* Guitarists: Tune lowest string to D.

me. _____

Fol-low me ____ up and down, _____ all ____ the way and all a - round, _____

Take my hand ____ and say you'll fol-low me. _____

It's long been on my mind, _____ you know it's
You see, I'd like to share my life with you ____ and

been a long, long time, I'll try to find the
show you things ____ I've seen, places that I'm

For You

Words and Music by John Denver

Just the words of a love song,_____ just the beat of my heart, just the pledge_of my life,_____ my love, for you.

Forever And Ever, Amen

Words and Music by Paul Overstreet and Don Schlitz

You may won - der how ___ I can
Well, hon - ey, I don't care, ___ I ain't in

prom - ise you now ___ if this love that I feel ___
love with your hair, ___ and if it all ___ fell out, ___

___ for you al - ways will be. ___ But
well, I'd love you an - y - way. ___ They say

you're not just time ___ that I'm kill - in'.
time can play tricks ___ on a mem - 'ry,

I'm no long - er one _____ of those guys. _____
make peo - ple for - get _____ things they knew. _____

_____
_____ As sure as I live, _____
Well, it's eas - y to see _____

_____ this love that I give _____ is
_____ it's hap - pen - in' to me. _____ I've al -

gon - na be yours _____ un - til the day that I _____ die. _____
read - y for - got - ten ev - 'ry wom - an but _____ you. _____

I'm gon-na love _____ you for - ev-er and ev - er, for -

ev - er and ev - er, a - men.

They say

Give Me Forever (I Do)

Words and Music by Carter Cathcart,
John Tesh, Juni Morrison and James Ingram

Looking out,_____ I see,_____ and I
With this ring_____ I'm bound,_____ and I

90

Coda

Am   D/F#

F   G

do.   To love you, I love you, I

Freely

Am   D/F#

F   G

do.   To love you, I love you, I do.

Tempo I

C   Fmaj7   Bb   Dm7

C   Fmaj7   Bb   Dm7   Cadd2

rit.

91

Theme from KARATE KID PART II

Glory Of Love

Words and Music by David Foster,
Peter Cetera and Diane Nini

Lyrics:
To - night it's ver - y clear, as we're both stand - ing here,

there's so man - y things I want to say.

I will al-ways love you, ___ I will nev-er leave you ___ a-lone. ___

Some-times I just for-get, say things I might re-gret, ___
You keep me stand-ing tall, you help me through it all, ___

it breaks my heart ___ to see ___ you cry - ing.
I'm al-ways strong ___ when you're ___ be - side me.

I don't want to lose you,___ I could nev-er make it___ a-lone.___
I have al-ways need-ed___ you, I could nev-er make it___ a-lone.___

I am a man who would fight

for your hon-or, I'll be the he-ro you're___ dream-ing of.___

We'll live for-ev-___ er, know-ing to-geth-___ er that we did it all for the glo-

94

Grow Old With Me

Words and Music by John Lennon

Have I Told You Lately

Words and Music by Van Morrison

ease my trou-bles, that's __ what you do.

For the
Instrumental solo

morn - in' sun in all __ its glo - ry

greets the

day with hope and com - fort, too. __

You fill my life with laugh - ter

and some-how you make it bet - ter,

from the Warner Bros. Film PURE COUNTRY

I Cross My Heart

Words and Music by Steve Dorff and Eric Kaz

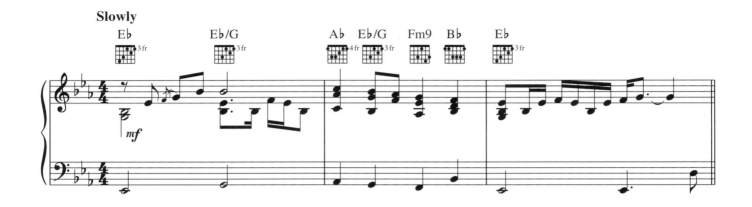

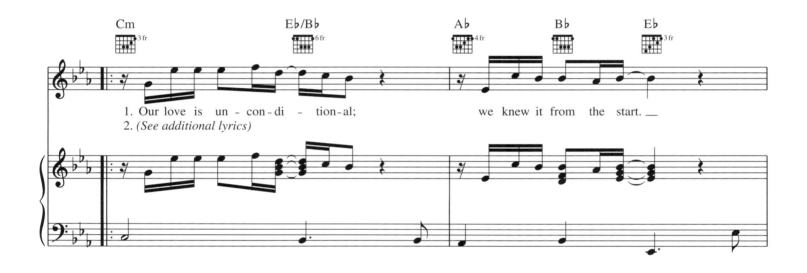

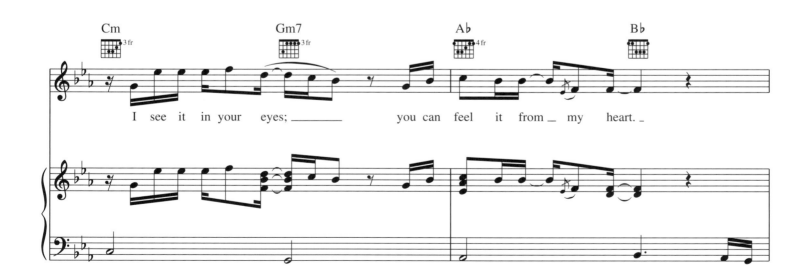

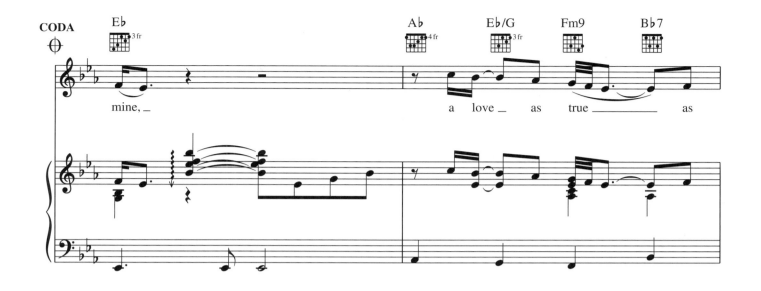

mine, __ a love __ as true _____ as

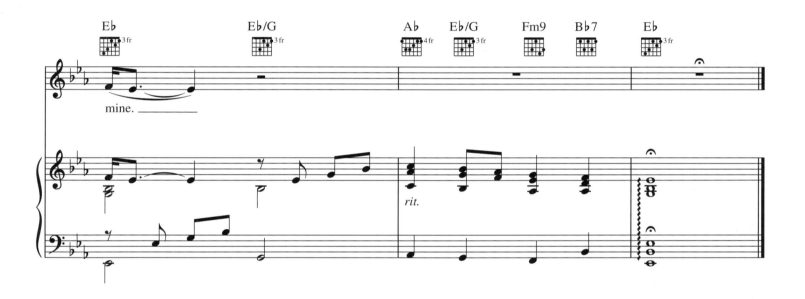

mine. _____

Additional Lyrics

2. You will always be the miracle
   That makes my life complete;
   And as long as there's a breath in me,
   I'll make yours just as sweet.
   As we look into the future,
   It's as far as we can see,
   So let's make each tomorrow
   Be the best that it can be.
   (To Chorus:)

from THE MIRROR HAS TWO FACES

I Finally Found Someone

Words and Music by Barbra Streisand, Marvin Hamlisch,
Robert Lange and Bryan Adams

Male: I fi-n'lly found some-one who knocks me off my feet.

I fi-n'lly found the one ___ that makes me feel com-plete.

Female: It start-ed o-ver cof-fee. We start-ed out as friends.

Cm7

It's fun-ny how from sim-ple things ___ the best things be-gin. ___

Cm7/F

G

Male: This time it's dif-f'rent.

Em7

It's all be-cause of you. ___

Cmaj7

It's bet-ter than it's ev - er been ___

Cm

'cause we can talk it through.

G(add9)

Female: My fav-'rite line ___

Em7

was, "Can I call you some - time?" ___

ev - er I do, ___ *Male:* it's just got to be you. *Both:* My

life has just be - gun. I fi - n'lly found some - one. ___

Male: Did I keep you wait - ing? I a - pol - o - gize. ___
Female: I did - n't mind. ___ Ba - by, that's fine. ___

I would wait for-ev - er just to know____ you were mine.____ You know,
just to know____ you were mine.____

I love your hair.____ I love what you wear.
Are you sure it looks right?____ Is-n't it too tight?____

____ You're ex - cep - tion - al. *Both:* I can't wait for the rest of my life.

This is it. Oh, _____ I fi - n'lly

I Swear

Words and Music by
Frank Myers and Gary Baker

from DIRTY DANCING

(I've Had)

The Time Of My Life

Words and Music by Franke Previte,
John DeNicola and Donald Markowitz

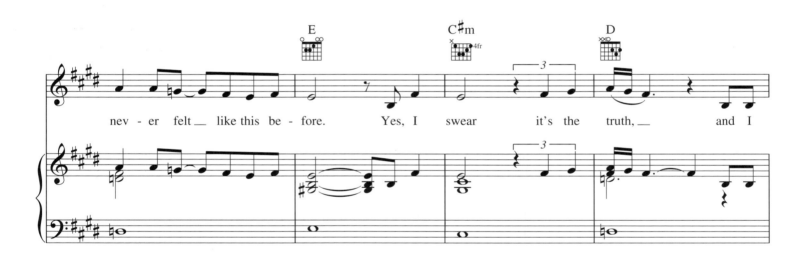

owe it all to you. _____

Male: I've been wait-ing for so long; _____ now I've

fi - n'lly found some-one __ to stand by me. *Female:* We saw the

writ - ing on the wall _____ as we felt this mag - i - cal __ fan - ta -

E

sy. _____

Both: Now   with

D/E

pas - sion in our eyes _____ there's no way we could _ dis - guise _____ it se - cret -

E

ly. _____

So   we

D/E

take each oth - er's hand _____ 'cause we seem to un - der - stand _ the ur - gen -

fore.   Yes, I   swear   it's the   truth, _____   and I   owe it all to   you. _____

_____   Male: Hey, ba - by.

Female: With   my   bod - y   and soul, _____   I   want   you

more   than you'll ev   -   er   know. _   Male: So we'll

just let it go; __ don't be a - fraid to lose con - trol. __

Female: Yes, I know what's on __ your mind when you say stay with me to-

night. __ *Male:* Stay __ with me. Just re - mem - ber, you're the

one thing __ *Female:* I __ can't get e - nough of. *Male:* So I'll tell you

some - thing: ___   *Both:* this could be love.   Be - cause   I've ___ had ___
                                                                                     I've

___   the time of my   life. ___   No, I nev - er felt ___ this way be -
had   the time of my   life. ___   And I've   searched through ev -'ry o - pen

fore.   Yes, I   swear   it's the   truth, _____   and I
door   till I've   found   the ___   truth, _____   and I

owe it all to you. ___ 'Cause   owe it all to you. _____

130

The Irish Wedding Song

Words and Music by Ian Betteridge

Lyrics under staff:

(T)Here they stand, hand in hand, they've ex-changed wed-ding
May they find peace of mind comes to all who are
As they go, may they know ev-'ry love that was

bands. To - day is the day of all their dreams and their
kind. May the rough times a - head be - come tri - umphs in
shown. And as life, it gets short - er, may their feel - ings

Just The Two Of Us

Words and Music by Ralph MacDonald, William Salter and Bill Withers

Moderately
Guitar → Cmaj7
(capo 1st fret)
Piano → D♭maj7
B7
C7
Em
Fm
Dm7
E♭m7
G7
A♭7
mp
Cmaj7
D♭maj7
B7
C7
Em7
Fm7
Cmaj7
D♭maj7
B7♯5
C7♯5
Em
Fm
Dm7
E♭m7
G7
A♭7
Cmaj7
D♭maj7
B7♯5
C7♯5
Em7
Fm7
Cmaj7
D♭maj7
B7
C7
Em
Fm
Dm7
E♭m7
G7
A♭7
I see the crys - tal rain - drops fall, and the beau - ty of it
We look for love; no time for tears. Wast - ed wa - ter's all that
I hear the crys - tal rain - drops fall on the win - dow down the
mf

cas-tles in—— the sky.—— Just the two of us, you and I.——

from the Broadway Musical THE WEDDING SINGER

It's Your Wedding Day

Words and Music by Matthew Sklar and Chad Beguelin

love is _____ what I _____ do.
love is _____ what I _____ do.

Robbie, Sammy & George:
Now, when we play a wed - ding gig, we're like a

fine - ly tuned _ ma - chine. ____

Robbie: Sam - my does Van Ha -

len licks _ while George _ gets down on tam - bou - rine. __

143

L-O-V-E

Words and Music by
Bert Kaempfert and Milt Gabler

L is for the way you look at me,

O is for the on-ly one I see.

V is ver-y, ver-y ex- tra- or-di-na- ry.

Love Of A Lifetime

**Words and Music by Bill Leverty
and Carl Snare**

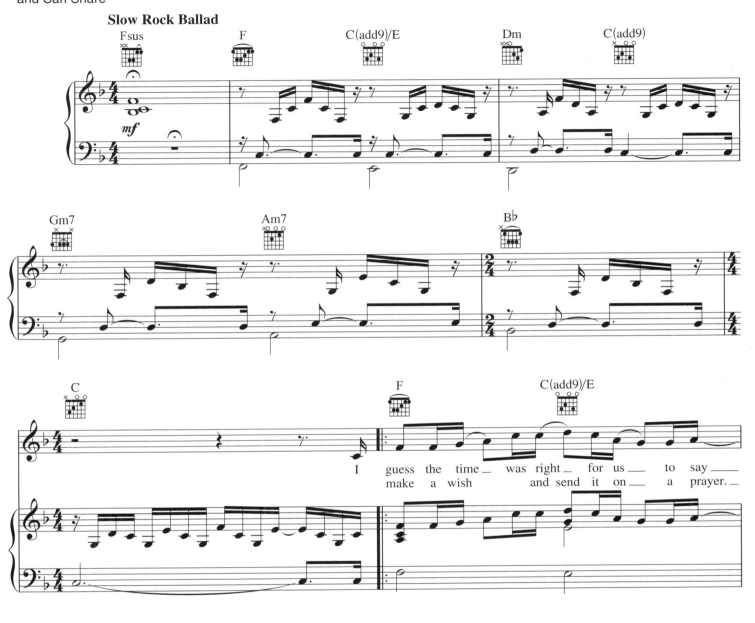

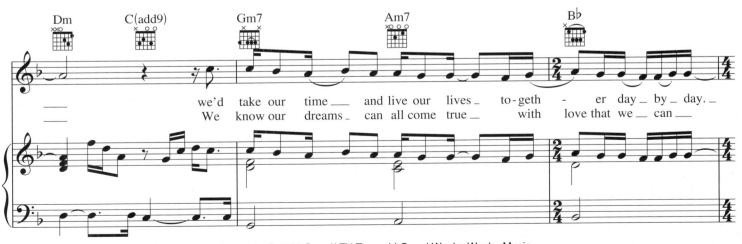

With ev-'ry kiss,__ our love__ is like__ brand - new__

and ev-'ry star__ up in__ the sky__ was made__

__ for me __ and you. __   Still, we both __ know that __ the road __ is long, __   but we

know that we __ will __ be __ to - geth - er __ be - cause our love __ is _____ strong. __   I

D.S. al Coda

154

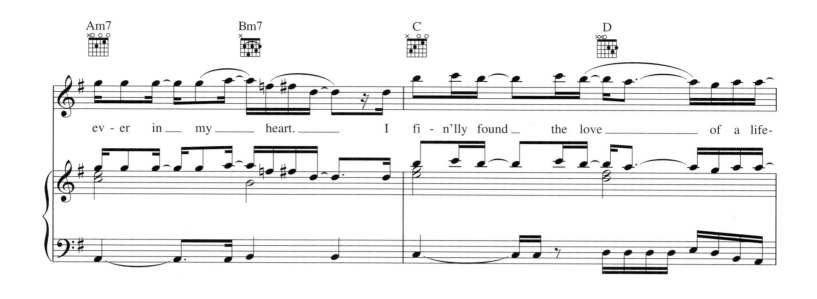

ev - er in my ____ heart. ____ I fi - n'lly found ____ the love ____ of a life-

- time, ____
(Fi - n'lly found ____ the love ____ of a life - time.)
love ____ of a life-

- time. ____
(Fi - n'lly found ____ the love ____ of a life - time.)
I fi - n'lly found ____ the love. ____

(Fi - n'lly found ___ the love ___ of a life - time,)   ooh,   for -

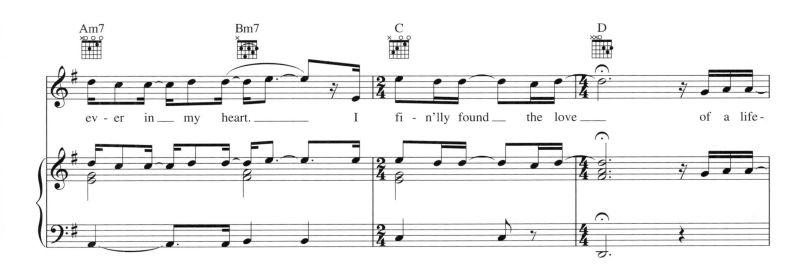

ev - er in ___ my heart. ___ I fi - n'lly found ___ the love ___ of a life -

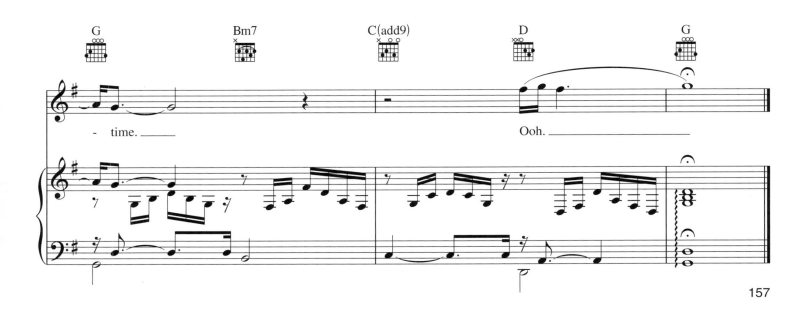

- time. ___   Ooh. _____

A Love Until The End Of Time

Music by Lee Holdridge
Words by Carol Connors

from DO RE MI

Make Someone Happy

Words by Betty Comden and Adolph Green
Music by Jule Styne

lights when it nears you, one {man}{girl} you're ev - 'ry - thing

to. Fame, _____ if you win it, comes and goes _

_ in a min - ute. Where's the real _ stuff in life to cling

to? Love _____ is the an - swer, some - one to

May You Always

Words and Music by Larry Markes and Dick Charles

Moderately, in tempo

Chorus:

of this day. I wish I may, I wish I might Have this wish I wish for you to - night. May you al - ways walk in sun - shine, slum - ber warm when night winds blow. May you al - ways live with laugh - ter for a smile be - comes you so. May good for - tune find your door - way, may the blue - bird sing your song. May no trou - ble

My Sweet Lady

Words and Music by John Denver

Lyrics:

La - dy, ___ are you cry - ing, ___ do the tears be - long to ___ me?
La - dy, ___ are you hap - py, ___ do you feel the way I ___ do?
La - dy, ___ are you cry - ing, ___ do the tears be - long to ___ me?

Did you think our time to - geth - er ___ was all gone?
are there mean - ings that you've nev - er ___ seen be - fore?
Did you think our time to - geth - er ___ was all gone?

La - dy, ___ you've been my sweet
La - dy, ___ my sweet
La - dy, ___ my sweet

stay right here be - side you. To -

day our lives were joined, be-came en - twined. I

wish that you could know how much I love you.

you.

D.S. al Coda

CODA

gun.

Never Gonna Let You Go

Words and Music by Barry Mann and Cynthia Weil

I'll re-gret ____ that ____ move ____ for as long as I'm liv-in'. ____
Oh, you gave ____ it ____ all ____ and I took it for grant- ____ ed. ____

But now that I've come ____ to see ____ the light, ____
But if there's some feel- ____ ing left ____ in you, ____

all I wan-na do ____ is make ____ things ____ right. So just
some flick-er of love ____ that still ____ shines ____ through, let's

say ____ the word ____ and tell me that I'm ____ for-giv- ____ en. And
talk ____ it out. ____ Let's talk a-bout sec- ____ ond chanc- ____ es. And

171

never gon-na let you go.____ I'm gon-na hold____ you in my arms for-ev-

-er. Gon-na try____ and make up for the times____ I hurt you so.____

Gon - na hold your bod-y close to mine.____

____ From this day on,____ we're gon-na be to-geth - er. Oh, I

swear this time, __ I'm nev-er gon-na let you go. _____

from JEKYLL & HYDE

A New Life

Words by Leslie Bricusse
Music by Frank Wildhorn

Moderately slow, freely

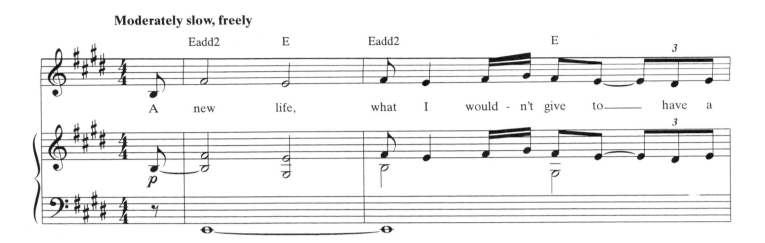

A new life, what I would-n't give to____ have a

new life! One thing I have learned as I go

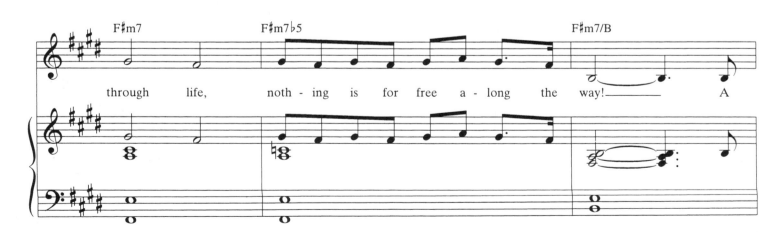

through life, noth-ing is for free a-long the way!____ A

new start, that's the thing I need to give me

new heart. Half a chance in life_____ to find a

new part, just a sim - ple role that I can

play._____ A new hope, some - thing_____ to con - vince me_____ to re -

new hope!   A

new day, bright e-nough to help me find my way!   A

new chance, one that may-be has a touch of ro-mance.

Where can it be,_____ the chance for me?   A

Moderately, in rhythm

new dream, I have one I know that ___ ver - y

few dream! I would like to see that ___ o - ver -

due dream, e - ven though it nev - er may come

true! A new love,

though I know there's no such___ thing as true love.

E - ven so, al - though I_____ nev - er knew love,

still I feel that one dream_ is my due!

A new world, this one thing I want to___ ask of you, world.

from JEKYLL & HYDE

Once Upon A Dream

Words by Steve Cuden and Leslie Bricusse
Music by Frank Wildhorn

Moderately

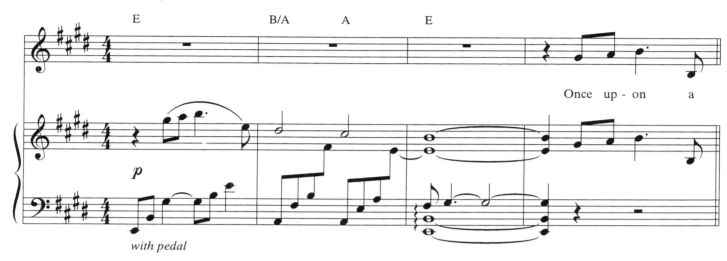

time   like no oth - er time be - fore.

Hope was still an o - pen door,   once up - on a

dream.   And I was un - a - fraid, the dream was so ex - cit - ing! But

now I see it fade and I am here a - lone!

One In A Million You

Words and Music by Sam Dees

Love had played its games on me so long ____ I start-ed to ____ be-lieve ____ I'd nev-er find ____ an-y-one. ____ Doubt had tried ____

and oh, what a rev-e-la-tion to see some-one was say-ing, "I love you" to me. A one in a mil-lion, chance of a life-time. And life showed com-

pas - sion _____ and sent to me a stroke of love called

you, _____ a one in a mil - lion you. _____

___ I was a lone - ly man _ with emp - ty arms _ to fill, _

___ then I found _ a piece _ of hap - pi - ness _ to

Open Arms

Words and Music by Steve Perry and Jonathan Cain

Perhaps Love

Words and Music by John Denver

love to some is like a cloud, to some as strong as steel. For

some a way of liv - ing, for some a way—— to feel 1.2. And

some say love is hold - ing on,—— and some say let - ting go. And

some say love is ev - 'ry-thing, some say they don't know. Per - haps

*Sing harmony
2nd time only.

198

from JEKYLL & HYDE

Someone Like You

Words by Leslie Bricusse
Music by Frank Wildhorn

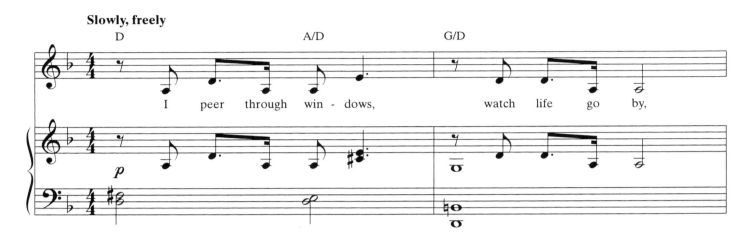

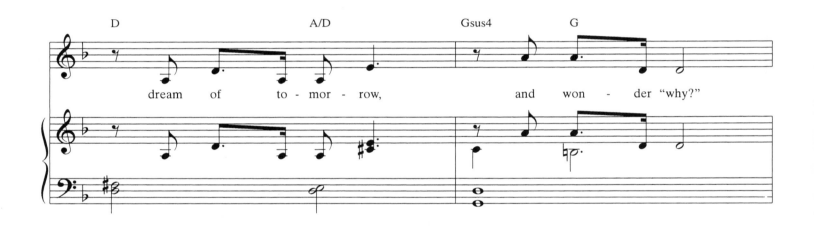

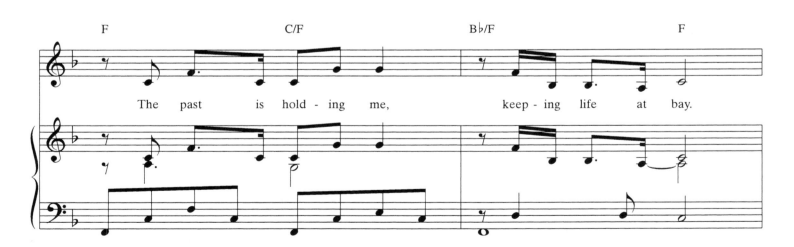

feel so a - live,_____ if some - one like you_____ found me!

So man - y se - crets I long to share! All I have need - ed is some - one there to help me see a world

ev - er be the same! There'd be a new way to live____ a

new life to love,____ if some - one like you____ found

me! Oh, if some - one____ like you found

some - one____ like me, then sud - den - ly____ noth - ing would

Stay The Same

Words and Music by Joe Carrier
and Joe McIntyre

way you are,__ ex-act-ly. Don't you ev-er say__ you don't

like the way__ you are. When you learn to love__ your-self,__ you're

bet-ter off__ by far. And I hope you al-ways stay the__ same,__

'cause there's noth-ing 'bout you I would__

To Coda

change. Be - lieve in___ your - self,___ reach down___ in - side.___ The love___ you find___ will set___ you free.___ Be - lieve in your - self,___ you will come___ a - live.___ Have faith in what___ you do,___

you'll make it through,_____ whoa,_____ hey!

Chorus:

Don't you ev - er wish you were___ some - one else.___ You were

meant to be_____ the way you are,___ ex - act - ly.

Don't you ev - er say_____ you don't like the way___ you are. When you

210

learn to love___ your-self,___ you're bet-ter off___ by far. And I

hope you al-ways stay the same,_____ 'cause there's

noth-ing 'bout you I would_____ change.___ No, there's

noth-ing 'bout you I would_____ change.

This I Promise You

Words and Music by Richard Marx

from GOYA

Till I Loved You

Music and Lyrics by Maury Yeston

Three Times A Lady

Words and Music by Lionel Richie

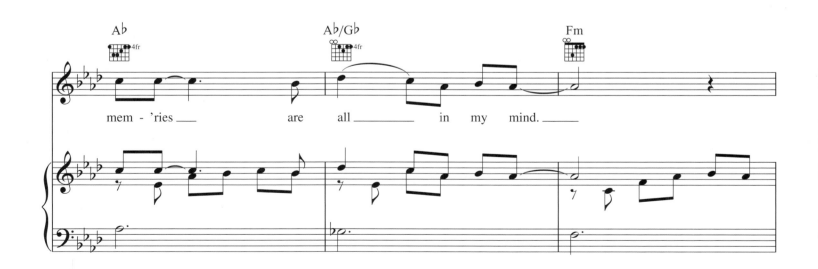

Tonight, I Celebrate My Love

Music by Michael Masser
Lyric by Gerry Goffin

Slowly and expressively

Unforgettable

Words and Music by Irving Gordon

how the thought of you does things ___ to me. Nev - er be - fore ___

has some - one been more ___ un - for - get - ta - ble, ___ in ev - 'ry way, ___

and for - ev - er - more, ___ that's how you'll

stay. _____ That's why, dar - ling,

it's in - cred - i - ble, that some - one so un - for - get - ta - ble

thinks that I am un - for - get - ta - ble, too.

too. _____

Truly

Words and Music by
Lionel Richie

Slowly

Girl, tell me on-ly this, that I have your heart for al - ways, and you want me by your side whis-per-ing the words "I'll al - ways

Now, I need to tell you this, there's no oth-er love like you, love. And I, as long as I live I'll give you all the joy my heart and

The Vows Go Unbroken (Always True To You)

Words and Music by Gary Burr and Eric Kaz

wave   of pure   de - vo - tion   has ___ swept   me off   my ___
goes   with - out   say -   ing,   but I'll   say   it   an - y -
die   be - fore   I'd   dam -   age   this ___ u - nion we have ___

feet.   And to - way.   To next strain   The

made.   The   vows   go ___ un - bro - ken.   And

you ___ still ___ know   I   do   love,   keep ___ and

241

Waiting For A Girl Like You

Words and Music by Mick Jones and Lou Gramm

love that will__ sur-vive._____ I've been wait - ing for

some-one new__ to make me feel_ a-live.___ Yeah, wait-ing__ for a

girl like you__ to come in-to__ my life.___

To Coda ✛

247

You're so good._____ When we make love__ it's un-

der - stood.__ It's more than a touch__ or a word__ we say.__

On - ly in dreams__ could it be____ this way._____ When you

love some-one,__ yeah,__ real-ly love some-one.__

from SWING TIME

The Way You Look Tonight

Words by Dorothy Fields
Music by Jerome Kern

We've Only Just Begun

Words and Music by Roger Nichols and Paul Williams

254

255

When I Fall In Love

Words by Edward Heyman
Music by Victor Young

give my heart; _____ And the

mo - ment I can feel that you feel that way

too is when I fall in love with you. _____

you. _____

When I Need You

Words and Music by Carole Bayer Sager
and Albert Hammond

Moderately, with feeling

When I need you, I just close my eyes and I'm with you, and all that I so want to give you, it's on-ly a heart-beat a-way. When I

from the Original Motion Picture BEACHES

The Wind Beneath My Wings

Words and Music by Larry Henley and Jeff Silbar

I nev-er once___ heard you com-plain.

Did you ev-er know___ that you're my___ he-ro,

and ev-'ry-thing___ I'd like to be?

I can fly high___ - er than an ea - gle,___

'cause you are the wind___ be-neath my wings.

It might have ap-peared___ to go un-

no - ticed that I've got it all___ here in my heart.

I want you to know___ I know the

You And I

Words and Music by
Frank Myers

Moderately slow

your love is my __ re - ward, __ and I love you e - ven more __ than

I ev - er did __ be - fore. __

I ev - er did __ be - fore. __

We made it, you __ and I.

rit.

You Are My Lady

Words and Music by Barry Eastman

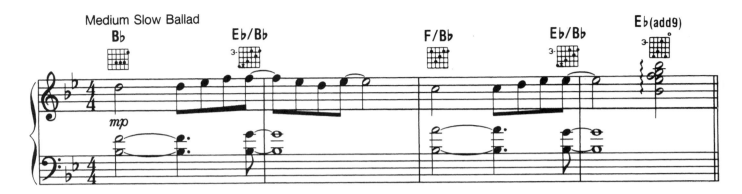

There's some-thing that I ___ want to say, ___ but words some-times get
There's no way that I ___ can re-sist ___ your ___ pre-

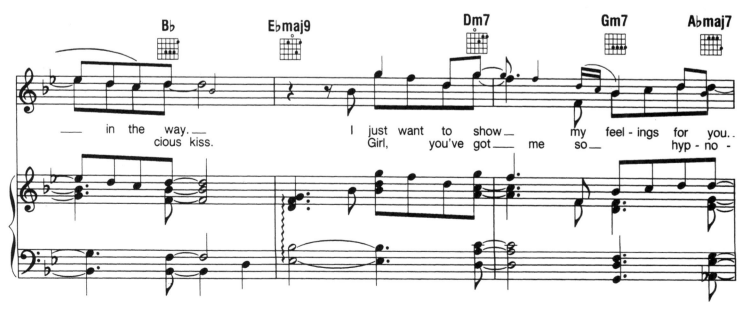

___ in the way. ___
cious kiss.

I just want to show ___ my feel-ings for you. ___
Girl, you've got ___ me so ___ hyp-no-

You Are So Beautiful

Words and Music by Billy Preston and Bruce Fisher

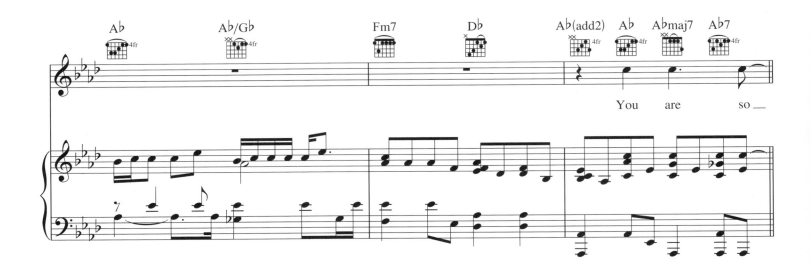

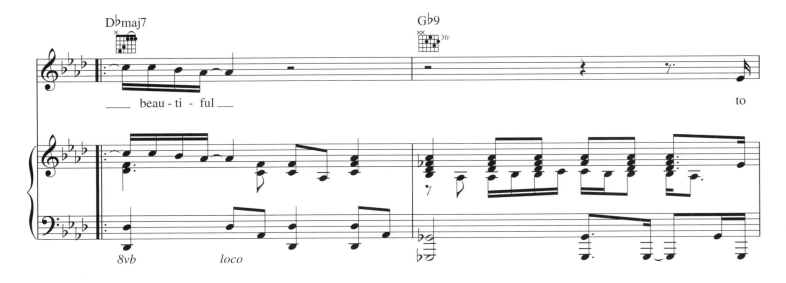

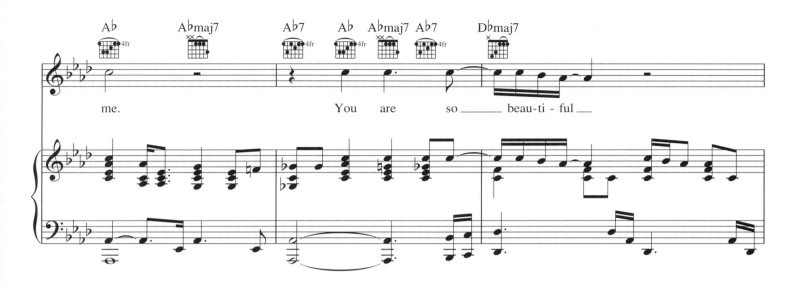

me.   You are so _____ beau-ti - ful _____

to me.   Can't you

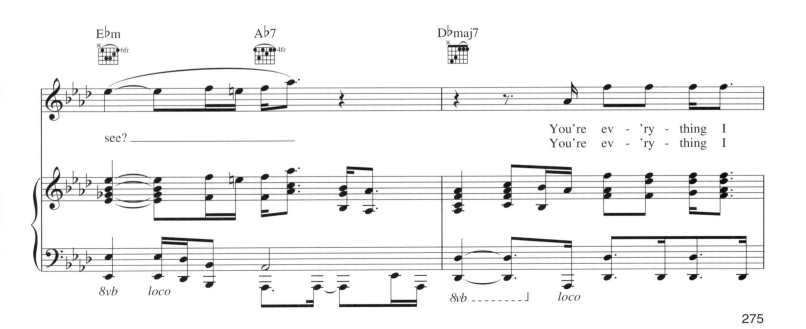

see? _____

You're ev - 'ry - thing I
You're ev - 'ry - thing I

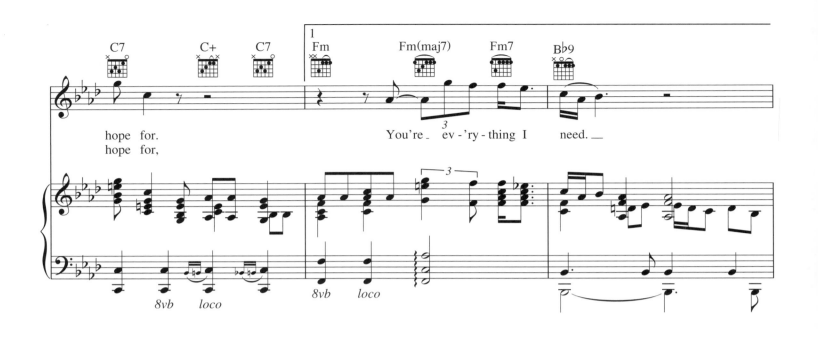

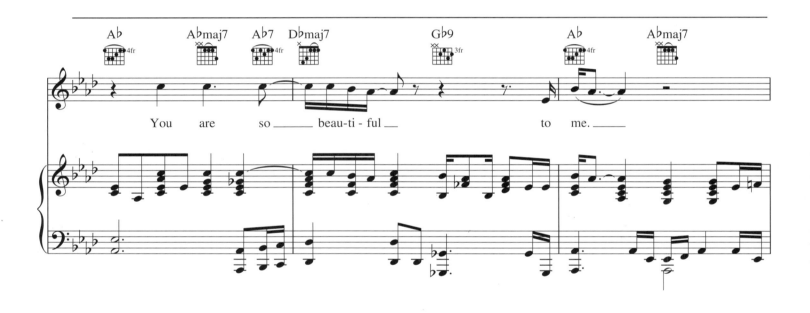

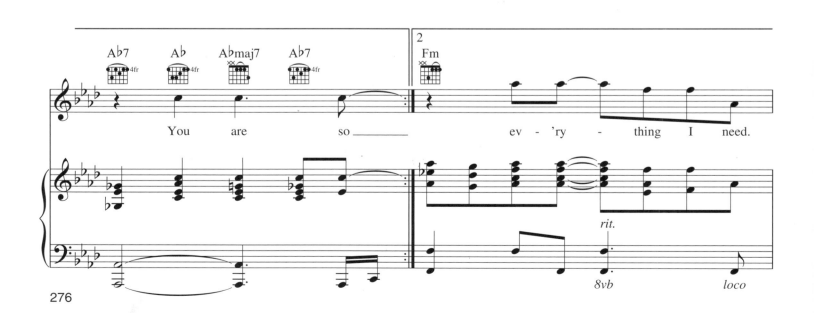

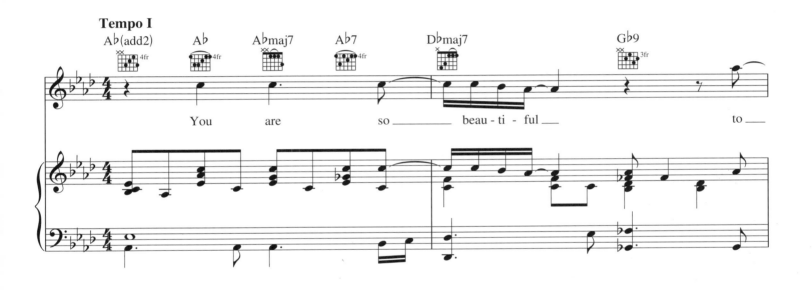

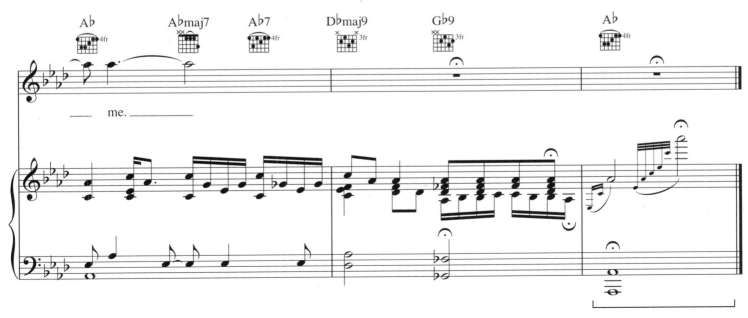

More Great Piano/Vocal Books

FROM CHERRY LANE

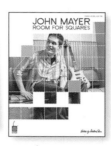

For a complete listing of Cherry Lane titles available,
including contents listings, please visit our web site at

www.cherrylane.com